EMMANUEL JOSEPH

The Mapmakers of Tomorrow,
Billionaires Who Redraw Industries and
Redefine the World Order

Copyright © 2025 by Emmanuel Joseph

All rights reserved. No part of this publication may be reproduced, stored or transmitted in any form or by any means, electronic, mechanical, photocopying, recording, scanning, or otherwise without written permission from the publisher. It is illegal to copy this book, post it to a website, or distribute it by any other means without permission.

First edition

This book was professionally typeset on Reedsy.
Find out more at reedsy.com

Contents

1. Chapter 1: The Genesis of Modern Titans — 1
2. Chapter 2: The Digital Frontiers — 3
3. Chapter 3: Pioneering Sustainable Futures — 5
4. Chapter 4: Redefining Health and Biotechnology — 7
5. Chapter 5: The Fintech Revolution — 9
6. Chapter 6: Education for the Future — 11
7. Chapter 7: The Future of Transportation — 13
8. Chapter 8: Transforming Communication — 15
9. Chapter 9: The Rise of Artificial Intelligence — 17
10. Chapter 10: Redefining Media and Entertainment — 19
11. Chapter 11: Shaping the Future of Work — 21
12. Chapter 12: The Impact of Philanthropy — 22
13. Chapter 13: Transforming Urban Landscapes — 23
14. Chapter 14: The Evolution of Retail — 24
15. Chapter 15: The Future of Food and Agriculture — 25
16. Chapter 16: Bridging the Gap in Energy and Resources — 27
17. Chapter 17: Legacy and Impact — 29
18. Chapter 17: Legacy and Impact — 30

1

Chapter 1: The Genesis of Modern Titans

The dawn of the 21st century marked an epoch in human history where the influence of technology began to seep into every crevice of society. Visionaries emerged, not merely as businessmen, but as architects of an impending revolution. This chapter delves into the inception of trailblazers who dared to dream beyond conventional boundaries. We explore their humble beginnings, where ideation often stemmed from garages and dorm rooms, to the realization that they possessed the unique ability to anticipate the trajectory of global needs. These individuals were not content with marginal improvements; they sought to redefine the very essence of industries.

Among these titans, names like Elon Musk, Jeff Bezos, and Jack Ma began to surface. Their stories were not just about accruing wealth, but about the relentless pursuit of disruptive innovation. Musk, with his audacious vision of interplanetary colonization, challenged the orthodoxy of space exploration. Bezos, through Amazon, transformed the retail landscape, making consumer convenience a pivotal axis. Ma, with Alibaba, revolutionized e-commerce in the East, bridging the gap between technology and traditional commerce. Together, these individuals exemplified the spirit of modern titans.

Their journeys were riddled with obstacles and skepticism. Musk's SpaceX faced numerous rocket failures, Bezos's Amazon was once deemed a financial black hole, and Ma encountered repeated rejections before Alibaba's breakthrough. However, their resilience and unyielding belief in their visions propelled them forward. The convergence of innovative thought and indomitable spirit laid the foundation for their monumental successes.

These pioneers did not merely seek personal glory; they envisioned a world where their innovations could elevate humanity. Their stories serve as a testament to the power of vision and the capacity to transcend limitations. As we delve deeper, we will uncover how these modern titans continue to redraw industries and redefine the world order, shaping the future in ways previously unimaginable.

2

Chapter 2: The Digital Frontiers

The digital revolution ushered in an era where information became the new gold. This chapter explores how billionaires harnessed the power of the internet and digital platforms to create vast empires. We examine the rise of social media magnates like Mark Zuckerberg, who transformed the way we connect and communicate. Facebook, initially a college networking site, burgeoned into a global social media behemoth, influencing political landscapes and societal norms.

Zuckerberg's journey is emblematic of the digital era's potential and pitfalls. His vision of connecting the world was not without controversy, as issues of privacy and data security surfaced. Despite these challenges, Facebook's impact on global communication cannot be understated. It became a catalyst for social movements, a marketplace for businesses, and a repository of human interaction on an unprecedented scale.

Similarly, Larry Page and Sergey Brin, the co-founders of Google, redefined how we access information. Their search engine revolutionized the internet, making vast amounts of knowledge accessible at our fingertips. Google's influence extended beyond search, with ventures into artificial intelligence, autonomous vehicles, and healthcare, illustrating the breadth of their ambition to shape the future.

The digital frontiers also witnessed the rise of e-commerce giants. Bezos's Amazon is a prime example of leveraging digital infrastructure to create a global retail empire. By prioritizing customer experience and utilizing data analytics, Amazon redefined consumer expectations and set new standards for the industry. This chapter elucidates how these digital pioneers reshaped the world, setting the stage for future innovations.

3

Chapter 3: Pioneering Sustainable Futures

As the world grappled with the realities of climate change, a new breed of billionaires emerged, committed to pioneering sustainable futures. This chapter delves into the initiatives of individuals like Bill Gates, who transitioned from technology mogul to global philanthropist. Gates's foundation invested heavily in renewable energy, healthcare, and education, addressing some of the most pressing challenges facing humanity.

Elon Musk, with Tesla and SolarCity, became a symbol of the green revolution. Tesla's electric vehicles challenged the dominance of fossil fuels, while SolarCity aimed to make solar energy accessible to the masses. Musk's vision extended to building a sustainable future on Earth and beyond, with SpaceX's ambitions of making humanity a multiplanetary species.

This chapter also explores the efforts of lesser-known but equally impactful figures like Yvon Chouinard, the founder of Patagonia. Chouinard's commitment to environmental stewardship and sustainable business practices set a precedent in the apparel industry. Patagonia's initiatives, from using recycled materials to advocating for conservation, demonstrated that profitability and sustainability could coexist.

The chapter underscores the importance of innovation in addressing global challenges. These billionaires' efforts in pioneering sustainable futures highlight a paradigm shift where wealth and influence are leveraged for the greater good. Their work serves as a blueprint for future leaders aiming to create a more equitable and sustainable world.

4

Chapter 4: Redefining Health and Biotechnology

The quest for better health and longevity has always been a driving force for humanity. This chapter explores how modern billionaires are revolutionizing the healthcare and biotechnology sectors. We begin with the story of Dr. Patrick Soon-Shiong, a medical entrepreneur whose groundbreaking work in cancer treatment has saved countless lives. His innovations in immunotherapy and personalized medicine have redefined the approach to healthcare, shifting from one-size-fits-all treatments to tailored therapies.

Bill Gates, through the Bill & Melinda Gates Foundation, has been instrumental in addressing global health challenges. From eradicating diseases like polio to improving sanitation in developing countries, Gates's philanthropic efforts have had a profound impact on global health. His investments in vaccine research and development during the COVID-19 pandemic exemplify his commitment to improving health outcomes worldwide.

Another key figure in this chapter is Elizabeth Holmes, the controversial founder of Theranos. Holmes's vision of revolutionizing blood testing captivated the world, but the company's eventual downfall serves as a cautionary tale about the importance of transparency and scientific integrity in biotechnology. While her story is a stark contrast to others in this book, it underscores the complexities and ethical considerations inherent in medical innovation.

We also explore the work of Dr. Craig Venter, a pioneer in genomics and synthetic biology. Venter's contributions to mapping the human genome and creating synthetic life forms have opened new frontiers in biotechnology. His work promises to revolutionize medicine, agriculture, and environmental sustainability, offering glimpses into a future where biotechnology plays a central role in shaping our world.

5

Chapter 5: The Fintech Revolution

The financial technology (fintech) sector has undergone a seismic transformation in recent years, driven by innovative billionaires who saw the potential to disrupt traditional banking and financial services. This chapter explores the rise of fintech giants like Jack Dorsey, the co-founder of Twitter and Square. Dorsey's vision of democratizing financial services through technology has empowered small businesses and individuals, providing them with tools for financial inclusion and growth.

Similarly, the story of Stripe, founded by brothers Patrick and John Collison, highlights the impact of fintech on global commerce. Stripe's platform simplified online payments, enabling businesses of all sizes to participate in the digital economy. The Collison brothers' relentless focus on improving the user experience and their commitment to fostering entrepreneurship have made Stripe a linchpin in the fintech ecosystem.

We also examine the rise of peer-to-peer lending platforms, such as LendingClub and Prosper, which have disrupted traditional lending by connecting borrowers directly with investors. These platforms have democratized access to credit, offering an alternative to traditional banks and fostering financial inclusion. Their success underscores the potential of fintech to create more equitable financial systems.

Cryptocurrencies and blockchain technology, pioneered by visionaries like Satoshi Nakamoto and Vitalik Buterin, have also played a transformative role in the fintech revolution. Bitcoin, the first cryptocurrency, challenged the very foundations of traditional finance, while Ethereum's smart contracts opened new possibilities for decentralized applications. This chapter delves into the impact of these technologies, highlighting their potential to reshape the future of finance.

6

Chapter 6: Education for the Future

Education is the cornerstone of societal progress, and modern billionaires have recognized the need to revolutionize this sector to prepare for the future. This chapter explores the efforts of individuals like Sal Khan, the founder of Khan Academy, who has democratized education through online platforms. Khan's vision of providing free, world-class education to anyone, anywhere, has empowered millions of learners across the globe.

Similarly, the story of Laurene Powell Jobs, through her Emerson Collective, highlights the importance of education reform. Powell Jobs has invested in innovative educational models that prioritize personalized learning and student-centered approaches. Her efforts to address educational inequities and support underserved communities underscore the transformative potential of education.

We also examine the work of Bill Gates, who has been a vocal advocate for improving education through technology. The Bill & Melinda Gates Foundation has invested heavily in initiatives to enhance teaching and learning, from developing digital tools to supporting research on effective educational practices. Gates's commitment to education reflects his belief in its power to drive societal progress.

This chapter underscores the importance of education for the future, highlighting how modern billionaires are leveraging their resources and influence to create more equitable and effective educational systems. Their efforts serve as a reminder that education is not just about imparting knowledge but about empowering individuals to reach their full potential.

7

Chapter 7: The Future of Transportation

Transportation has always been a critical factor in shaping civilizations, and modern billionaires are at the forefront of revolutionizing how we move. This chapter explores the contributions of individuals like Elon Musk, whose ventures in electric vehicles and space travel are pushing the boundaries of what's possible. Tesla's electric cars have redefined the automotive industry, while SpaceX's reusable rockets promise to make space travel more accessible and sustainable.

We also examine the work of Travis Kalanick, the co-founder of Uber, whose ride-hailing platform disrupted traditional taxi services and changed the way we think about transportation. Uber's success has spurred the rise of the success of other ride-hailing services like Lyft, and has led to a broader conversation about the future of urban mobility.

In addition, we explore the role of Richard Branson and his ventures in space tourism with Virgin Galactic. Branson's ambition to make space travel accessible to the public represents a new frontier in transportation, where the boundaries of our planet are no longer limitations. His work highlights the potential for private space exploration to complement governmental efforts and push the envelope of human exploration.

This chapter also touches on the advancements in public transportation, such as high-speed rail and hyperloop technologies, which promise to revolutionize how we travel long distances. These innovations, driven by individuals like Elon Musk and companies like Hyperloop One, aim to make transportation faster, more efficient, and environmentally friendly.

The future of transportation is being shaped by visionary billionaires who see beyond the status quo. Their efforts are not just about building faster cars or rockets, but about reimagining how we move and connect as a society. As we continue to explore their contributions, we will see how their innovations are setting the stage for a new era of transportation.

8

Chapter 8: Transforming Communication

The way we communicate has undergone a dramatic transformation in recent years, thanks to the efforts of modern billionaires who have harnessed the power of technology to connect people across the globe. This chapter explores the contributions of individuals like Elon Musk, who through SpaceX's Starlink project, aims to provide global internet coverage using a network of satellites. This initiative has the potential to bring connectivity to remote and underserved regions, bridging the digital divide.

We also examine the impact of social media platforms, such as Twitter, founded by Jack Dorsey. Twitter has become a global platform for real-time communication, enabling users to share information, engage in discussions, and mobilize social movements. Its influence on public discourse and its role in shaping the news cycle underscore the transformative power of digital communication.

Mark Zuckerberg's Facebook and its subsidiaries, Instagram and WhatsApp, have also played a pivotal role in transforming how we communicate. These platforms have created new avenues for social interaction, business marketing, and political engagement. However, they have also raised important questions about privacy, data security, and the ethical use of technology.

This chapter highlights the ways in which modern billionaires are leveraging technology to transform communication. Their innovations are not just about creating new tools, but about redefining how we connect, share, and interact in an increasingly digital world.

9

Chapter 9: The Rise of Artificial Intelligence

Artificial intelligence (AI) is poised to be one of the most transformative technologies of the 21st century, and modern billionaires are at the forefront of its development and implementation. This chapter explores the contributions of individuals like Elon Musk and his company, OpenAI, which aims to ensure that artificial general intelligence (AGI) benefits all of humanity. Musk's advocacy for responsible AI development and his warnings about the potential risks of AI underscore the importance of ethical considerations in this field.

Similarly, Sundar Pichai, the CEO of Alphabet Inc., has been instrumental in advancing AI technologies through Google. Google's AI research and development have led to significant breakthroughs in natural language processing, computer vision, and autonomous systems. Pichai's vision of integrating AI into various aspects of daily life reflects the potential of this technology to enhance human capabilities and improve quality of life.

This chapter also examines the work of Demis Hassabis, the co-founder of DeepMind, whose AI research has achieved remarkable milestones, such as defeating world champions in the game of Go and making advances in protein folding predictions. Hassabis's work highlights the potential of AI to solve complex scientific problems and contribute to advancements in healthcare, climate science, and more.

The rise of AI presents both opportunities and challenges. This chapter delves into the ways in which modern billionaires are navigating this landscape, balancing innovation with ethical considerations to ensure that AI benefits society as a whole.

10

Chapter 10: Redefining Media and Entertainment

The media and entertainment industry has undergone significant changes in recent years, driven by the vision and innovation of modern billionaires. This chapter explores the contributions of individuals like Reed Hastings, the co-founder of Netflix, whose platform has revolutionized the way we consume content. Netflix's transition from a DVD rental service to a global streaming giant has reshaped the entertainment landscape, influencing how we watch movies, TV shows, and documentaries.

Similarly, Jeff Bezos's acquisition of The Washington Post highlights the intersection of technology and journalism. Under Bezos's ownership, the newspaper has embraced digital transformation, leveraging technology to enhance reporting, reach new audiences, and sustain its business model in the digital age.

We also examine the work of Rupert Murdoch, whose media empire spans newspapers, television networks, and film studios. Murdoch's influence on the media landscape is profound, shaping public opinion and political discourse through his vast array of media outlets.

This chapter delves into the ways in which modern billionaires are redefining media and entertainment. Their efforts are not just about creating new platforms or content, but about reshaping how we access, consume, and engage with media in an increasingly digital world.

11

Chapter 11: Shaping the Future of Work

The nature of work is evolving rapidly, influenced by technological advancements and the vision of modern billionaires who are redefining industries and business models. This chapter explores the contributions of individuals like Tim Cook, the CEO of Apple, whose leadership has driven the company's innovation in products and services, creating new job opportunities and transforming the tech industry.

Similarly, Satya Nadella, the CEO of Microsoft, has played a pivotal role in advancing cloud computing, artificial intelligence, and productivity tools. Under Nadella's leadership, Microsoft has become a leader in enterprise solutions, empowering businesses and workers to thrive in the digital age.

We also examine the impact of gig economy platforms, such as Uber and Airbnb, which have created new forms of work and income opportunities. While these platforms offer flexibility and convenience, they also raise important questions about labor rights, job security, and the future of work.

This chapter highlights the ways in which modern billionaires are shaping the future of work. Their innovations are not just about creating new technologies, but about reimagining how work is organized, performed, and rewarded in an increasingly digital and interconnected world.

12

Chapter 12: The Impact of Philanthropy

Philanthropy has become a significant avenue for modern billionaires to effect positive change and address global challenges. This chapter explores the philanthropic efforts of individuals like Warren Buffett, who has pledged the majority of his wealth to charitable causes through The Giving Pledge. Buffett's commitment to philanthropy reflects his belief in the power of wealth to create meaningful and lasting impact.

Similarly, Bill and Melinda Gates have become synonymous with philanthropic leadership. Their foundation has made significant contributions to global health, education, and poverty alleviation. The Gates Foundation's investments in vaccine development, disease eradication, and educational reform exemplify their dedication to improving the lives of people around the world.

We also examine the philanthropic initiatives of Michael Bloomberg, whose charitable contributions have focused on public health, climate change, and education. Bloomberg's support for initiatives such as tobacco control, renewable energy, and educational innovation highlights his commitment to addressing pressing global issues.

This chapter underscores the importance of philanthropy in the lives of modern billionaires. Their efforts to give back to society demonstrate that wealth and influence can be harnessed for the greater good, creating a positive legacy for future generations.

13

Chapter 13: Transforming Urban Landscapes

Urbanization is a defining trend of the 21st century, and modern billionaires are playing a pivotal role in shaping the future of cities. This chapter explores the contributions of individuals like Marc Lore, who has proposed creating a new city in the United States, designed to incorporate innovative urban planning, sustainable living, and advanced technology.

Similarly, Elon Musk's Boring Company aims to address urban congestion through the development of underground transportation tunnels. Musk's vision of reducing traffic and creating more efficient transportation systems highlights the potential of technology to transform urban landscapes.

We also examine the work of Jeff Bezos, whose Amazon headquarters in Seattle has had a profound impact on the city's economy and infrastructure. Amazon's presence has spurred economic growth, created jobs, and influenced urban development, reflecting the broader trend of tech companies shaping the future of cities.

This chapter delves into the ways in which modern billionaires are transforming urban landscapes. Their efforts to create more sustainable, efficient, and livable cities reflect their vision of a better future for urban communities.

14

Chapter 14: The Evolution of Retail

The retail industry has experienced significant disruption in recent years, driven by the vision and innovation of modern billionaires. This chapter explores the contributions of individuals like Jeff Bezos, whose company, Amazon, has revolutionized the retail landscape. Amazon's emphasis on customer experience, convenience, and data analytics has set new standards for the industry, influencing how consumers shop and how businesses operate.

Similarly, the story of Jack Ma and Alibaba highlights the impact of e-commerce on global trade. Alibaba's platforms have enabled small businesses to reach international markets, fostering entrepreneurship and economic growth. Ma's vision of leveraging technology to empower businesses and consumers has transformed the retail industry in China and beyond.

We also examine the rise of direct-to-consumer brands, which have disrupted traditional retail models by selling products directly to customers online. Companies like Warby Parker and Casper have leveraged digital platforms to build strong brand identities, engage with customers, and offer personalized shopping experiences.

This chapter delves into the evolution of retail, highlighting how modern billionaires are reshaping the industry. Their innovations are not just about creating new products or services, but about redefining the relationship between businesses and consumers in the digital age.

15

Chapter 15: The Future of Food and Agriculture

The future of food and agriculture is being shaped by modern billionaires who are leveraging technology to address global challenges and create more sustainable systems. This chapter explores the contributions of individuals like Bill Gates, whose investments in agricultural innovation aim to improve food security and support smallholder farmers in developing countries.

Similarly, Elon Musk, through his company SpaceX, has explored the potential of cultivating crops in space. His vision of interplanetary colonization includes sustainable food production, which is crucial for long-term space missions and habitation on other planets. Musk's work in this area highlights the intersection of space exploration and agricultural innovation.

This chapter also delves into the rise of alternative protein sources, such as lab-grown meat and plant-based substitutes. Visionaries like Pat Brown, the founder of Impossible Foods, and Ethan Brown, the founder of Beyond Meat, are revolutionizing the food industry with their innovative products. These companies aim to reduce the environmental impact of meat production and provide healthier, more sustainable alternatives to traditional animal agriculture.

Additionally, we explore the impact of vertical farming and precision agriculture, which utilize technology to optimize crop production and reduce resource consumption. Companies like Plenty and AeroFarms are leading the way in vertical farming, creating efficient, high-yield systems that can be implemented in urban environments. This chapter highlights how modern billionaires are driving the future of food and agriculture, ensuring that we can feed a growing population sustainably.

16

Chapter 16: Bridging the Gap in Energy and Resources

The quest for sustainable energy and resource management is a critical challenge of our time, and modern billionaires are at the forefront of this movement. This chapter explores the contributions of individuals like Elon Musk, whose work with Tesla and SolarCity aims to revolutionize the energy sector. Tesla's electric vehicles and energy storage solutions, combined with SolarCity's solar panels, represent a comprehensive approach to reducing our reliance on fossil fuels.

Similarly, Richard Branson's Virgin Group has invested in renewable energy projects and environmental initiatives. Branson's commitment to sustainability is evident in ventures like Virgin Galactic, which aims to make space travel more eco-friendly, and Virgin Voyages, which focuses on reducing the environmental impact of cruise travel.

We also examine the work of innovators in the field of clean energy, such as Bill Gates, whose Breakthrough Energy Ventures invests in cutting-edge technologies to address climate change. This chapter highlights how these billionaires are bridging the gap in energy and resources, ensuring a sustainable future for generations to come.

The chapter underscores the importance of collaboration and innovation in tackling global challenges. The efforts of modern billionaires in this space demonstrate that with the right resources and vision, we can create a more sustainable and equitable world. Their work serves as a testament to the power of innovation and the potential to transform our energy and resource systems for the better.

17

Chapter 17: Legacy and Impact

The final chapter of our journey examines the legacy and impact of the modern billionaires who have reshaped industries and redefined the world order. We explore the lasting contributions of individuals like Elon Musk, Jeff Bezos, Bill Gates, and others, whose visions have transcended their lifetimes and continue to influence future generations.

Their stories are not just about wealth accumulation, but about the enduring impact of their innovations and philanthropic efforts. From advancing technology and improving healthcare to fostering sustainability and empowering education, their contributions have left an indelible mark on society.

This chapter also reflects on the ethical considerations and responsibilities that come with great wealth and influence. The actions of these billionaires serve as a reminder that their decisions have far-reaching consequences, and their legacies are shaped by the choices they make.

As we conclude this book, we are reminded that the mapmakers of tomorrow are not just the billionaires who redraw industries, but the individuals who dare to dream big and act with purpose. Their stories inspire us to envision a better future and take action to create a world that benefits all of humanity.

18

Chapter 17: Legacy and Impact

The final chapter of our journey examines the legacy and impact of the modern billionaires who have reshaped industries and redefined the world order. We explore the lasting contributions of individuals like Elon Musk, Jeff Bezos, Bill Gates, and others, whose visions have transcended their lifetimes and continue to influence future generations.

Their stories are not just about wealth accumulation, but about the enduring impact of their innovations and philanthropic efforts. From advancing technology and improving healthcare to fostering sustainability and empowering education, their contributions have left an indelible mark on society.

This chapter also reflects on the ethical considerations and responsibilities that come with great wealth and influence. The actions of these billionaires serve as a reminder that their decisions have far-reaching consequences, and their legacies are shaped by the choices they make.

As we conclude this book, we are reminded that the mapmakers of tomorrow are not just the billionaires who redraw industries, but the individuals who dare to dream big and act with purpose. Their stories inspire us to envision a better future and take action to create a world that benefits all of humanity.

The Mapmakers of Tomorrow: Billionaires Who Redraw Industries and Redefine the World Order

CHAPTER 17: LEGACY AND IMPACT

In the 21st century, a new breed of visionaries has emerged, reshaping industries and redefining the world order. "The Mapmakers of Tomorrow" takes you on a captivating journey through the lives of modern billionaires who are not just amassing wealth, but are architects of profound change. From the digital revolution spearheaded by Mark Zuckerberg and Larry Page, to the green revolution championed by Elon Musk and Bill Gates, this book delves into the stories of those who dared to dream beyond the conventional.

Discover how these pioneers, armed with relentless ambition and innovative prowess, have transformed sectors such as healthcare, fintech, transportation, and communication. Uncover the ethical dilemmas and responsibilities they face as they navigate the complexities of their immense influence. Through chapters filled with detailed narratives and thought-provoking insights, this book highlights the enduring impact of their contributions on society.

"The Mapmakers of Tomorrow" is not just a chronicle of success; it is an exploration of the visionary spirit that drives these billionaires to create a better future. Their stories serve as an inspiration to envision a world where innovation and purpose go hand in hand. Join us in understanding how these modern titans are crafting the blueprint for a new era, and how their legacy will shape the generations to come.

www.ingramcontent.com/pod-product-compliance
Lightning Source LLC
LaVergne TN
LVHW020503080526
838202LV00057B/6126